ROYAL COURT

Royal Court Theatre presents

ALMOST NOTHING
and AT THE TABLE

by Marcos Barbosa
translated by Mark O'Thomas

First performance at the Royal Court Jerwood Theatre Upstairs
Sloane Square, London on 5 February 2004.

ALMOST NOTHING and AT THE TABLE are presented as part of the International Playwrights
Season 2004, a Genesis Project with additional support from the British Council.

INTERNATIONAL PLAYWRIGHTS SEASON 2004

A Genesis Project

5 - 27 March 2004
LADYBIRD by **Vassily Sigarev** translated by Sasha Dugdale
Directed by Ramin Gray

LADYBIRD is Vassily Sigarev's third play produced by the Royal Court. Previous productions were PLASTICINE (International Playwrights Season 2002) and BLACK MILK (Focus Russia 2003). Sigarev won the 2002 Evening Standard Charles Wintour Award for Most Promising Playwright.

Monday - Saturday 7.45pm | Saturday matinees 4pm
Press nights Monday 8 and Tuesday 9 March | Sign-interpreted performance Thursday 18 March

10 - 11 March
STATES OF VIOLENCE
Readings of specially comissioned plays responding to the subject of violence by writers from countries including Argentina, Brazil, China, Germany, India, Serbia, Sweden, Palestine, Ukraine and the USA.

12 March
THE STATE OF PALESTINE
A one day seminar on recent developments in Palestine, including readings of work by young Palestinian writers.

13 March
CITY STATES
Readings of short plays by five Royal Court writers who have travelled to cities around the world to work with international playwrights:

April De Angelis, HAVANA; David Greig, RAMALLAH; Stephen Jeffreys, KAMPALA
Mark Ravenhill, MOSCOW; Roy Williams, SÃO PAULO

30 March - 3 April 2004
CUBA REAL New Plays from Cuba
In the last two years the Royal Court has collaborated with the National Council of Scenic Arts (CNAE) in Cuba to run writers' groups for emerging playwrights. Since September 2002 Royal Court practitioners have made three visits to Cuba, working with ten playwrights in Escambray, Cienfuegos and Matanzas. Now in specially commissioned translations, we present rehearsed readings of five new plays from this on-going collaboration. The plays offer a rare insight into contemporary Cuba. There are additional events on Cuban culture and history, and a chance to enjoy Cuban music, food and drink.

For full details please contact the Box Office on 020 7565 5000.

International Playwrights Season 2004 is supported by the Genesis Foundation and additional support from the British Council.

The Genesis Foundation is committed to long-term support for the Royal Court's Young Writers Festival as well as its International Season. These are initiatives that find, develop and promote work by emerging writers. The aim of these programmes is to provide means whereby young, talented writers can become the next generation of professional playwrights. Genesis helps the Royal Court offer a springboard to greater public and critical attention. Genesis is committed to process, not completion.

For more information see:
http://www.genesisfoundation.org.uk

ALMOST NOTHING
and AT THE TABLE

by **Marcos Barbosa**
translated by Mark O'Thomas

Cast in order of appearance
ALMOST NOTHING
Antonio **Ewan Stewart**
Sara **Nina Sosanya**
Vania **Lorna Gayle**
Casar **Karl Johnson**

AT THE TABLE
Castro **Karl Johnson**
Inacio **Jonathan Timmins**
Father **Ewan Stewart**
Bruno **Robert Timmins**
Marcio **Mido Hamada**
Luis **Mark Bonnar**

Director **Roxana Silbert**
Designer **Anthony MacIlwaine**
Lighting Designer **Chahine Yavroyan**
Sound Designer **Matt McKenzie**
Assistant Director **Tiffany Watt-Smith**
Casting **Lisa Makin**
Production Manager **Sue Bird**
Stage Managers **Linsey Hall, Sally Higson**
Costume Supervisor **Iona Kenrick**
Company Voice Work **Patsy Rodenburg**

There will be a fifteen minute interval between the two plays.

THE COMPANY

Marcos Barbosa (writer)
Marcos Barbosa comes from Fortaleza, Brazil and took part in a new writers' group in São Paulo run by the Royal Court in association with the British Council in April 2001. His short play ALMOST THREE was produced as part of the Royal Court's International Season 2002. He attended the Royal Court's International Residency 2002 on a British Council scholarship, developing his play ALMOST NOTHING, presented as a rehearsed reading in New Plays from Brazil in January 2003. ALMOST NOTHING premiered at the Teatro Popular do SESI in São Paulo, September 2003.

Mark Bonnar
Theatre includes: Twelfth Night, The Cherry Orchard, Robin Hood, Richard III, Out in the Open, The Country Wife, Tales from Ovid, Volpone. Anthony & Cleopatra, Richard III, Flight, Chips with Everything, The Seal Wife.
Television includes: Taggart, Wire in the Blood, Loving You, Armadillo, Inspector Rebus, The Phoenix and the Carpet.

Lorna Gayle
Graduated from Webber Douglas Academy, March 2003.
Theatre includes: Stepping Out (Southwold Summer Theatre).
Television includes: Canterbury Tales, The Bill, Baby Mother.

Mido Hamada
For the Royal Court: Spinning into Butter.
Other theatre includes: A View from the Bridge (West Yorkshire Playhouse/Birmingham Repertory Theatre); Yerma (Young Vic); A Dark River (The Bigger Picture Company & tour).
Television and film includes: World of Tomorrow, Believe Nothing, Make My Day, Light, Bouncers.
Radio includes: On the Piste.

Karl Johnson
For the Royal Court: Caryl Churchill season, The Night Heron, Boy Gets Girl, The Weir, Been So Long, Just a Little Less than Normal, Sudlow's Dawn, Irish Eyes and English Tears.
Other theatre includes: Tales from the Vienna Woods, Scenes from the Big Picture, The Walls, Cardiff East, The Ends of the Earth, The Machine Wreckers, Black Snow, The Resistible Rise of Arturo Ui, The Sea, Uncle Vanya, A Midsummer Night's Dream, Glengarry Glen Ross, Wild Honey, The Mysteries, Tim Page's Nam, Don Quixote, The Shape of the Table, The Rivals (RNT); In the Company of Men, TV Times, Knight of the Burning Pestle (RSC); Amadeus (Peter Hall Company); Woyzeck (Lyric, Hammersmith); War Crimes (ICA); The Dresser (Thorndike, Leatherhead); Hedda Gabler (Yvonne Arnaud, Guildford); As You Like It (Old Vic), Vieux Carre (Piccadilly).
Television includes: England Expects, Born and Bred, The Mayor of Casterbridge, Dalziel and Pascoe, Without Motive, David Copperfield, Vanity Fair, The Temptation of Franz Schubert, Wing and a Prayer, An Independent Man, As You Like It, Catherine the Great, Lifeboat, Glassing Gareth, Judas and The Gimp, Sexual Intercourse Began in 1963, The Shawl, A Tale of Two Cities, Rules of Engagement, Poirot, Casualty, The Bill, Boon, Bergerac, Sons and Lovers, Rock Follies of 77, Chips With Everything.
Film includes: Frozen, Pure, Tomorrow La Scala, Love is the Devil, Wittgenstein, Close My Eyes, Prick Up Your Ears, Jubilee, The Tempest, The Tent, The Magic Shop, Soup.

Anthony MacIlwaine (designer)
For the Royal Court: Iron (Traverse Theatre production).
Theatre includes: Cinderella (Lyric, Hammersmith); 15 Seconds, Quartz (Traverse); The Mikado (Grange Park Opera); Making Noise Quietly (Oxford Stage Company); Wozzeck, From the House of Dead (Long Beach Opera); Beauty and the Beast (Young Vic); Prayers of Sherkin (Old Vic); Euripides Trilogy, Aurelie My Sister, Danton's Death, Agamemnon's Children, The Lovers, The Cheating Hearts (Gate); Peribanez (Arts Theatre, Cambridge); Loot (Magnificent Theatre Co); Dark Ride (SoHo Rep, New York); Grimm Tales (Leicester Haymarket); Await the Tide (Edinburgh Festival).

Matt McKenzie (sound designer)

For the Royal Court: Iron (Traverse Theatre production).

Theatre includes: Favourite Nights, Rents, Britannicus, Noises Off, The White Glove, The Provoked Wife, Private Dick, Miss Julie, Hobson's Choice, Mass Appeal, Crime And Punishment, Lent, The Man Who Fell In Love With His Wife, Angry Housewives, The Hypochondriac, Faith Hope And Charity, Sailor Beware, Loot, Lady Audley's Secret, Madras House, The Way of the World, Ghost Train, Greasepaint, In the Summer House, Exact Change (Lyric Hammersmith); Macbeth, Love Off The Shelf (Nuffield, Southampton); Una Pooka (Tricycle); Vertigo, Hinge of the World (Guildford); Easy Virtue, The Seagull (Chichester); People Next Door (Traverse); Made In Bangkok, The House Of Bernarda Alba, A Piece Of My Mind, Journey's End, A Madhouse In Goa, Barnaby And The Old Boys, Irma Vep, Gasping, Map of the Heart, Tango Argentino, When She Danced, Misery, Murder Is Easy, The Odd Couple, Pygmalion, Things We Do For Love, Long Day's Journey Into Night (West End); Lysistrata, The Master Builder, School For Wives, Mind Millie For Me, A Streetcar Named Desire, Three Of A Kind, Amadeus (Peter Hall); Frame 312, After Miss Julie (Donmar); The Family Reunion, Henry V, The Duchess Of Malfi, Hamlet, The Lieutenant Of Inishmore, Julius Caesar, A Midsummer Night's Dream (RSC). Matt was Sound Supervisor for the Peter Hall Seasons at The Old Vic and Piccadilly and designed sound for Waste, Cloud 9, The Seagull, The Provok'd Wife, King Lear, The Misanthrope, Major Barbara, Filumena, Kafka's Dick. Musicals include: Bells Are Ringing, Talk of the Steamie (Greenwich); Forbidden Broadway, Blues in the Night (West End); Car Man (West End and international tour); Putting It Together, The Gondoliers (Chichester); Oh What A Lovely War, A Christmas Carol (Derby Playhouse) and co-sound design of Tess (Savoy) and Alice In Wonderland (RSC).

Mark O'Thomas (translator)

As writer, theatre includes: Food for Thought (Soho); Salvador (Man in the Moon); Viva Maria!, OneFourSeven (Oval House); Down Dog (Edinburgh Festival 2003); The Piranha Lounge (Lyric Studio).

He has worked as translator and script adviser for the Royal Court since 2001.

Roxana Silbert (director)

Currently Literary Director of the Traverse, previously Associate Director at the Royal Court and the West Yorkshire Playhouse.

For the Royal Court: Iron (Traverse Theatre production); Been So Long, Fair Game, Bazaar, Sweetheart, Essex Girls, Mules, Wounds to Her Face, Voices for Nine (Barclays New Stages) and Artistic Director of Coming on Strong (Young Writers Festival 1994).

For the Traverse: Slab Boys (also national tour), People Next Door (also Stratford East), 15 Seconds, Green Field, Quartz.

Other theatre includes: Precious (West Yorkshire Playhouse); Splash Hatch on the E Going Down (Donmar); Cadillac Ranch (Soho); The Fast Show Live (Phil McIntyre Productions at the Apollo Hammersmith and national tour); A Servant of Two Masters (Crucible); Translations, Top Girls (New Vic); The Price (Bolton Octagon); Love (London Opera Festival); Two Horsemen (Bush/Gate); The Lovers (Gate); The Treatment (Intercity Festival, Florence); Backstroke in a Crowded Pool (National Theatre Pakistan/British Council); Animals of Farthing Wood (Green & Lenagan Productions at The Pleasance).

Television includes: Table Twelve Series (World Production for Channel 4).

Radio includes: Secret Life of a Bumble Bee, The Tall One, Brace Position.

Nina Sosanya

Theatre includes: As You Like It, The Learned Ladies, The White Devil (RSC); The Vortex (Donmar); Marriage of Figaro (Royal Exchange, Manchester); House & Garden, Antony & Cleopatra (RNT); The Nativity (Young Vic); Dead Meat (West Yorkshire Playhouse); The Tempest (Holders Festival, Barbados); Herbal Bed, Henry V (RSC tour); The Happy Haven (RSC Fringe); Educating Rita (Solent People's Theatre); Twelfth Night, A Midsummer Night's Dream, The Tempest (national & international tours); Othello (Baron's Court Theatre); Dinner Dance (KOSH national & international tours); Hair (European tour).

Television and film includes: Love Actually, Serious & Organised, The Debt, Teachers, The Jury, People Like Us, Doctors, Jonathan Creek, Prime Suspect 11, The Bill, Hercules and the Amazon Women.

Ewan Stewart
For the Royal Court: Our Late Night, Sacred
Heart, Trade, Bluebird, Thyestes, Live Like Pigs,
Road (& national tour), Flying Blind.
Other theatre includes: Green Field (Traverse);
Sisters, Brothers (Gate); The Duchess of Malfi
(Bristol Old Vic); A Working Woman (West
Yorkshire Playhouse); Phoenix (Bush); Racing
Demon, The Murderers, Major Barbara,
Serjeant Musgrave's Dance, A Month in the
Country, In the Blue, As I Lay Dying (RNT);
When We Were Women, Torquata Tasso (RNT
Studio); The Orphan's Comedy, Lucy's Play
(Traverse/Edinburgh Festival); Midsummer
Night's Dream (Scottish Opera).
Television includes: POW, The Key, Conspiracy,
Real Men, Touch and Go, Looking after Jo Jo,
Nervous Energy, A Mug's Game, Down Among
the Big Boys, Spender, The Bill, The Advocates,
Eurocops 111, Boon, Dream Baby, Only Fools
and Horses, Biting the Hand, Radical Chambers,
The Shutter Falls, Good and Bad at Games, A
Woman Calling, Antony and Cleopatra, Ill Fares
the Land, Green Street Revisited, Quiet Days of
Mrs Stafford, The Professionals, Mackenzie,
Barriers, Rain on the Roof, Shadows on our Skin,
The Camerons.
Film includes: The Bum's Rush, Young Adam,
The Last Great Wilderness, The Closer You Get,
Big Brass Ring, Titanic, Stella Does Tricks, Rob
Roy, Kafka, Flight to Berlin, The Cook, The
Thief, His Wife and Her Lover, Resurrected,
Paradise Postponed, Not Quite Jerusalem,
Remembrance, Who Dares Wins, All Quiet on
the Western Front.

Jonathan Timmins
Television includes: Let's Write a Story, Murder
in Mind, Inspector Lynley Mysteries.
Film includes: Wimbledon (Summer 2004), The
Prince & the Pauper.

Robert Timmins
Television includes: Little Friends, Great Britons,
Oscar Charlie.
Film includes: The Prince & the Pauper.

Tiffany Watt-Smith (assistant director)
Tiffany is Associate Director at Arcola Theatre.
As assistant director, for the Royal Court: Blood.
As assistant director, other theatre includes:
Coriolanus (RSC Swan).
As director, theatre includes: Kismet, Mud,
Venezuela, Trash, Teatro X La Identidad
(Arcola).
Tiffany also works as a freelance writer for film
and television.

Chahine Yavroyan (lighting designer)
For the Royal Court: Iron, Outlying Islands (both
Traverse Theatre productions), The Lying Kind,
Bazaar, One More Wasted Year, Stranger's
House.
Other theatre includes: 15 Seconds, Green
Fields, Gagarin Way, Anna Weiss, Knives in Hens,
The Speculator, Perfect Days, King of the Fields,
Wiping My Mother's Arse, Shining Souls, The
Architect (Traverse); Stitching, Darwin's Flood,
Shang-A-Lang (Bush); Edward Gant's Amazing
Feats of Loneliness (Drum); Wolk's World,
Hedda Gabler (Royal Exchange, Manchester);
Cosmonaut's Last Message, San Diego (Tron);
Pygmalion, Othello (Nottingham Playhouse);
South Pacific, Villette, King Lear (Sheffield
Crucible); La Musica Deuxiemme, Gaucho
(Hampstead); Variete (Lindsay Kemp);
Tantamount Esperance, Standing Room Only
(Rose English); An Die Musik (Pip Simmons).
Dance includes: Yolande Snaith Theatredance,
Rosemary Lee, Anatomy Dance, Bock &
Vincenzi, Naheed Saddiqui, Walkerdance, Colin
Poole, Bedlam, Yasmin Vardimon, Arthur Pita.
Site-specific work includes: Station House
Opera, Dreamwork at St. Pancras Chambers,
Spa at Elizabeth Garrett-Anderson Hospital,
Coin Street Museum, Red Earth, Push, The City
of Bologna New Year's Eve celebrations.
Fashion shows for Givenchy, Chalayan, Clemens-
Ribeiro, Ghost.
Other: Michael Moore Live, Jocelyn Pook's
Speaking Tongues, Mango Lick for Mannafest, A
Better Place for ENO. Long-standing People
Show person.

THE ENGLISH STAGE COMPANY AT THE ROYAL COURT

The English Stage Company at the Royal Court opened in 1956 as a subsidised theatre producing new British plays, international plays and some classical revivals.

The first artistic director George Devine aimed to create a writers' theatre, 'a place where the dramatist is acknowledged as the fundamental creative force in the theatre and where the play is more important than the actors, the director, the designer'. The urgent need was to find a contemporary style in which the play, the acting, direction and design are all combined. He believed that 'the battle will be a long one to continue to create the right conditions for writers to work in'.

Devine aimed to discover 'hard-hitting, uncompromising writers whose plays are stimulating, provocative and exciting'. The Royal Court production of John Osborne's Look Back in Anger in May 1956 is now seen as the decisive starting point of modern British drama and the policy created a new generation of British playwrights. The first wave included John Osborne, Arnold Wesker, John Arden, Ann Jellicoe, N F Simpson and Edward Bond. Early seasons included new international plays by Bertolt Brecht, Eugène Ionesco, Samuel Beckett, Jean-Paul Sartre and Marguerite Duras.

The theatre started with the 400-seat proscenium arch Theatre Downstairs, and then in 1969 opened a second theatre, the 60-seat studio Theatre Upstairs. Some productions transfer to the West End, such as Terry Johnson's Hitchcock Blonde, Caryl Churchill's Far Away, Conor McPherson's The Weir, Kevin Elyot's Mouth to Mouth and My Night With Reg. The Royal Court also co-produces plays which have transferred to the West End or toured internationally, such as Sebastian Barry's The Steward of Christendom and Mark Ravenhill's Shopping and Fucking (with Out of Joint), Martin McDonagh's The Beauty Queen Of Leenane (with Druid Theatre Company), Ayub Khan-Din's East is East (with Tamasha Theatre Company, and now a feature film).

Since 1994 the Royal Court's artistic policy has again been vigorously directed to finding and producing a new generation of playwrights. The writers include Joe Penhall, Rebecca Prichard, Michael Wynne, Nick Grosso, Judy Upton, Meredith Oakes, Sarah Kane, Anthony Neilson, Judith Johnson, James Stock, Jez Butterworth, Marina Carr, Phyllis Nagy, Simon Block, Martin McDonagh, Mark Ravenhill, Ayub Khan-Din, Tamantha Hammerschlag, Jess Walters, Ché Walker, Conor McPherson, Simon Stephens, Richard Bean, Roy Williams, Gary Mitchell, Mick Mahoney, Rebecca Gilman, Christopher Shinn, Kia Corthron, David Gieselmann, Marius von Mayenburg, David Eldridge, Leo Butler, Zinnie Harris, Grae Cleugh, Roland Schimmelpfennig, DeObia Oparei, Vassily Sigarev, the Presnyakov Brothers and Lucy Prebble. This expanded programme of new plays has been made possible through the support of A.S.K Theater Projects and the Skirball Foundation, the Jerwood Charitable Foundation, the American Friends of the Royal Court Theatre and many in association with the Royal National Theatre Studio.

INTERNATIONAL PLAYWRIGHTS

Since 1992 the Royal Court Theatre has placed a renewed emphasis on the development of international work and a creative dialogue now exists with theatre practitioners all over the world including Brazil, Cuba, France, Germany, India, Palestine, Russia, Spain, and Uganda. All of these development projects are supported by the British Council and the Genesis Foundation.

The Royal Court has worked with playwrights and directors from Brazil since 1995 as part of its annual International Residency. In March 2000 the Royal Court made its first trip to Brazil with the support of the British Council. Since then Royal Court playwrights and directors have continued to travel to Brazil to work with emerging playwrights and collaborate with the Centro Cultural in São Paulo and Teatro Vila Velha in Salvador.

In January 2003 five Brazilian playwrights came to London to take part in a week of readings, NEW PLAYS FROM BRAZIL in the Jerwood Theatre Upstairs. In May 2003 a new phase of the work began with a group of writers at Centro Cultural in São Paulo. This was followed by a director's workshop at SESI in São Paulo and a new writer's group at Sala Paraíso, Teatro Carlos Gomez in Rio in November 2003.

International Playwrights Season is produced by the Royal Court International Department: Associate Director **Elyse Dodgson** International Administrator **Ushi Bagga** International Associate **Ramin Gray**

AWARDS FOR
THE ROYAL COURT

Jez Butterworth won the 1995 George Devine Award, the Writers' Guild New Writer of the Year Award, the Evening Standard Award for Most Promising Playwright and the Olivier Award for Best Comedy for Mojo.

The Royal Court was the overall winner of the 1995 Prudential Award for the Arts for creativity, excellence, innovation and accessibility. The Royal Court Theatre Upstairs won the 1995 Peter Brook Empty Space Award for innovation and excellence in theatre.

Michael Wynne won the 1996 Meyer-Whitworth Award for The Knocky. Martin McDonagh won the 1996 George Devine Award, the 1996 Writers' Guild Best Fringe Play Award, the 1996 Critics' Circle Award and the 1996 Evening Standard Award for Most Promising Playwright for The Beauty Queen of Leenane. Marina Carr won the 19th Susan Smith Blackburn Prize (1996/7) for Portia Coughlan. Conor McPherson won the 1997 George Devine Award, the 1997 Critics' Circle Award and the 1997 Evening Standard Award for Most Promising Playwright for The Weir. Ayub Khan-Din won the 1997 Writers' Guild Awards for Best West End Play and Writers' Guild New Writer of the Year and the 1996 John Whiting Award for East is East (co-production with Tamasha).

At the 1998 Tony Awards, Martin McDonagh's The Beauty Queen of Leenane (co-production with Druid Theatre Company) won four awards including Garry Hynes for Best Director and was nominated for a further two. Eugene Ionesco's The Chairs (co-production with Theatre de Complicite) was nominated for six Tony awards. David Hare won the 1998 Time Out Live Award for Outstanding Achievement and six awards in New York including the Drama League, Drama Desk and New York Critics Circle Award for Via Dolorosa. Sarah Kane won the 1998 Arts Foundation Fellowship in Playwriting. Rebecca Prichard won the 1998 Critics' Circle Award for Most Promising Playwright for Yard Gal (co-production with Clean Break).

Conor McPherson won the 1999 Olivier Award for Best New Play for The Weir. The Royal Court won the 1999 ITI Award for Excellence in International Theatre. Sarah Kane's Cleansed was judged Best Foreign Language Play in 1999 by Theater Heute in Germany. Gary Mitchell won the 1999 Pearson Best Play Award for Trust. Rebecca Gilman was joint winner of the 1999 George Devine Award and won the 1999 Evening Standard Award for Most Promising Playwright for The Glory of Living.

In 1999, the Royal Court won the European theatre prize New Theatrical Realities, presented at Taormina Arte in Sicily, for its efforts in recent years in discovering and producing the work of young British dramatists.

Roy Williams and Gary Mitchell were joint winners of the George Devine Award 2000 for Most Promising Playwright for Lift Off and The Force of Change respectively. At the Barclays Theatre Awards 2000 presented by the TMA, Richard Wilson won the Best Director Award for David Gieselmann's Mr Kolpert and Jeremy Herbert won the Best Designer Award for Sarah Kane's 4.48 Psychosis. Gary Mitchell won the Evening Standard's Charles Wintour Award 2000 for Most Promising Playwright for The Force of Change. Stephen Jeffreys' I Just Stopped by to See The Man won an AT&T: On Stage Award 2000.

David Eldridge's Under the Blue Sky won the Time Out Live Award 2001 for Best New Play in the West End. Leo Butler won the George Devine Award 2001 for Most Promising Playwright for Redundant. Roy Williams won the Evening Standard's Charles Wintour Award 2001 for Most Promising Playwright for Clubland. Grae Cleugh won the 2001 Olivier Award for Most Promising Playwright for Fucking Games. Richard Bean was joint winner of the George Devine Award 2002 for Most Promising Playwright for Under the Whaleback. Caryl Churchill won the 2002 Evening Standard Award for Best New Play for A Number. Vassily Sigarev won the 2002 Evening Standard Charles Wintour Award for Most Promising Playwright for Plasticine. Ian MacNeil won the 2002 Evening Standard Award for Best Design for A Number and Plasticine. Peter Gill won the 2002 Critics' Circle Award for Best New Play for The York Realist (English Touring Theatre). Ché Walker won the 2003 George Devine Award for Most Promising Playwright for Flesh Wound.

ROYAL COURT BOOKSHOP

The bookshop offers a wide range of playtexts and theatre books, with over 1,000 titles. Located in the downstairs Bar and Food area, the bookshop is open Monday to Saturday, afternoons and evenings.

Many Royal Court playtexts are available for just £2 including works by Harold Pinter, Caryl Churchill, Rebecca Gilman, Martin Crimp, Sarah Kane, Conor McPherson, Ayub Khan-Din, Timberlake Wertenbaker and Roy Williams.

For information on titles and special events, Email: bookshop@royalcourttheatre.com
Tel: 020 7565 5024

PROGRAMME SUPPORTERS

The Royal Court (English Stage Company Ltd) receives its principal funding from London Arts. It is also supported financially by a wide range of private companies and public bodies and earns the remainder of its income from the box office and its own trading activities.
The Royal Borough of Kensington & Chelsea gives an annual grant to the Royal Court Young Writers' Programme.

The Jerwood Charitable Foundation continues to support new plays by new playwrights through the Jerwood New Playwrights series. Since 1993 A.S.K. Theater Projects and the Skirball Foundation have funded a Playwrights' Programme at the theatre. Bloomberg Mondays, the Royal Court's reduced price ticket scheme, is supported by Bloomberg. Over the past seven years the BBC has supported the Gerald Chapman Fund for directors.

ROYAL COURT
SLOANE SQUARE

11 February - 20 February
Jerwood Theatre Downstairs

NOTES ON FALLING LEAVES

by Ayub Khan-Din

Directed by Marianne Elliott

A new short play by one of Britain's leading dramatists in a production without décor.

As his mother fades away, a son returns to the house where he grew up. It is empty but full of reminders of how she once was. She, meanwhile, has her own foggy memories and feelings about why they try, but just can't, communicate.

Cast: Pam Ferris and Ralf Little

Supported by

JERWOOD
NEW PLAYWRIGHTS

with additional support from
THE ROYAL COLLEGE OF PSYCHIATRISTS

BOX OFFICE 020 7565 5000
www.royalcourttheatre.com

ALMOST NOTHING

(*Quase Nada*)

Marcos Barbosa

translated into English by Mark O'Thomas

Characters

ANTÔNIO

SARA

VÂNIA

CÉSAR

Setting: the living room of Antônio and Sara's house.

1.

A long silence.

ANTÔNIO. Are you going to let me do all the talking?

She stares at him, without saying anything.

Nimbly, as a joke, he kisses her on the lips. She jumps and gets him back by playfully slapping his face.

Once again, he kisses her on the lips. Once again, she plays along and slaps him.

He hesitates a moment and then kisses her once more, receiving yet another slap in return.

Are you going to stop now?

SARA. Are *you* going to stop now?

After a moment's thought, he shakes his head. Without waiting for the kiss, she slaps him one more time. They both laugh.

Silence.

What time is it?

ANTÔNIO (*after checking his watch*). Almost three. Are you sleepy?

She nods.

Want to come and lie down with me?

SARA. Later.

ANTÔNIO. Didn't you say you were tired?

She nods.

So why don't you want to sleep, then?

Silence.

Are you angry with me?

She shakes her head.

So what is it, then?

She puts her fingers to his lips and stops him speaking. She pats her thighs and he lies down with his head on her lap.

SARA. Can you still hear it?

ANTÔNIO. What?

SARA. That noise, in your ear.

He nods.

ANTÔNIO. It comes and goes. It's as if . . . As if it's a bell of some kind. A silver bell tinkling away. I hear a bang and then a hum and then it goes down, getting softer and softer . . . And then it stops and things are OK for a while, as if it's nothing at all. But then it comes back all of a sudden, the same way, once again, the same thing: starting loud and then getting softer, like a bell, in a church, except the sound is clearer, more delicate, not like a bell-clapper, it's different to that, more like a small bell, like someone tapping a fork on a crystal glass, you know that sound? You know the keys of a piano – those at the end: right at the end, very tinny? That's what it's like. More or less. And it comes back again and again. Crash, softer, softer and then back again. At first I thought it was just my ear – this one here, just on this side. But no. It's both of them, at the same time. I hear a bang here, very close, as if it was just behind me, just behind my head and then the noise comes and gets softer and softer until it's just the distant humming sound. And then it all comes back.

SARA. And it isn't any better?

He shakes his head.

If it hasn't stopped hurting by the time you wake up tomorrow, we'll get you to the doctor's.

ANTÔNIO. It doesn't hurt.

SARA. What?

ANTÔNIO. The ear. It doesn't hurt.

SARA. But didn't you just say it did?

ANTÔNIO. No. Not the ear. It's just the noise. I hear a noise. There's no pain in the ear. The pain is here in my head, at the front. Do you think there's something wrong?

SARA. How do you mean?

ANTÔNIO. With the ear, because of the bang.

SARA. No. I was just next to you. I heard exactly the same noise as you did. It'll be gone tomorrow when you wake up.

ANTÔNIO. Will it?

SARA. Of course it will.

Silence.

ANTÔNIO. Right now, it's stopped. The noise.

SARA. Really?

He nods.

What did I tell you?

ANTÔNIO. It's like that all the time – it comes and goes.

Silence.

I love you.

A brief silence and she suddenly bursts out laughing.

What's wrong?

SARA (*regaining control of herself*). Nothing.

ANTÔNIO. What is it?

SARA. I love you, too.

They hold each other's hands. She tries to contain another bout of laughter but fails.

ANTÔNIO. What is it?

SARA (*regaining control*). Nothing.

ANTÔNIO. Tell me.

SARA. Nothing.

ANTÔNIO. Tell me.

She collapses into a fit of giggles once more, only now her laughter becomes contagious: they both laugh.

What is it?

SARA (*trying to control herself*). You were talking about your ear and then, out of the blue, came: 'I love you.'

They both laugh again. Eventually, the laughter dissipates.

ANTÔNIO. I love you.

Silence.

SARA. So what should we do?

ANTÔNIO. I don't know. What?

She does not reply.

SARA. Do you think something's going to happen?

ANTÔNIO. No. (*After a pause.*) Are you scared?

SARA. What of?

ANTÔNIO. Scared.

SARA. No. (*After a pause.*) You?

He shakes his head.

Silence.

ANTÔNIO. But there is something a bit odd.

SARA. How do you mean?

ANTÔNIO. Something funny, that doesn't feel right.

SARA. We did the right thing. And now it's over.

ANTÔNIO. Even so.

SARA (*patting her lap once more*). Come on, lie down.

He lies down.

Your eye's all red.

ANTÔNIO. It's the headache.

SARA. Don't you want to sleep?

ANTÔNIO. Yes, with you.

SARA. In a bit.

ANTÔNIO. I'll wait.

Silence.

You worry too much.

SARA. I haven't said a word.

ANTÔNIO. Why are you being like this?

SARA. I'm tired, I already told you.

ANTÔNIO. And I already said I was sorry.

SARA. I know.

Silence.

ANTÔNIO. You don't believe me.

SARA. I do. Of course I do. It's over and done with. In a little while, I'll go and sleep.

ANTÔNIO. You're angry.

She shakes her head.

Yes, you are.

Silence.

See?

SARA. What?

ANTÔNIO. You're angry.

Silence.

Let me look at you.

SARA. What for?

ANTÔNIO. Let me.

She turns away from his gaze.

Let me.

They stare at each other for a while, serious and resolute, but end up laughing at the seriousness of the other. Silence.

SARA. And what if they come after us?

ANTÔNIO. They won't. They've no way of finding us out.

SARA. But what if they do?

ANTÔNIO. They won't.

He lays down with his head on her lap. She strokes his hair.

SARA. There's something in your ear.

ANTÔNIO. What?

SARA. Let me see. Stay still.

She examines his ear carefully.

I can't see it properly.

ANTÔNIO. How come?

SARA. It's too dark now. I'll have a look tomorrow.

ANTÔNIO. What is it?

SARA. I can't see it properly.

ANTÔNIO. Try.

SARA. It's like a mark, a kind of blemish.

ANTÔNIO. Where?

SARA. Inside. Right down inside.

ANTÔNIO. It could be a shard or something from the shot. Couldn't it?

SARA. No. It's probably always been there. It's tiny.

ANTÔNIO. Look at the other one.

She looks at his other ear.

SARA. No. There's nothing in this one.

ANTÔNIO. Nothing?

SARA. Nothing. All normal.

ANTÔNIO. The noise is coming from both of them.

SARA. There's nothing in this one.

ANTÔNIO. There could be something wrong just this side even though I can hear the noise in both ears. At first, I thought it was coming from just the one ear.

SARA. Let me have another look. No. It's something of nothing. It was probably there before. If it was something bad, we wouldn't be having this conversation – you'd already be in hospital by now – you wouldn't be able to bear the pain. You did say it wasn't hurting.

ANTÔNIO. It's just the noise. It just hurts here at the front: a headache.

SARA. Well, then.

Silence.

ANTÔNIO. Did you see his face?

SARA. No.

ANTÔNIO. I did. It was all over in a flash but I can remember it. When you screamed and I saw that figure come up to the car, I couldn't tell what it was but when I pulled the trigger and fired, I saw him. It was all over so fast but I caught a glimpse. It was less than a second but it's still there. I think the shot got him in the eye – this eye here. He put his hand to his eye, like this. Or maybe it was the fall – as he fell, his hand could have flown up in front of his face. But it looked like he felt the bullet enter his head, through his eye, and he tried to cover the hole with his hand. Like this. All over in less than a second, but it's stayed with me. You saw it too, didn't you?

She shakes her head.

Nothing?

She shakes her head.

Silence.

SARA. His face.

ANTÔNIO. What about it?

Silence.

What about it?

SARA. I saw it. Well enough: close up, when he came to the window. It had a cut, here on the side. Wounded, here, on the cheek, this side. As if he'd been slashed.

ANTÔNIO. By the shot?

SARA. No, from before.

Silence.

I think I could smell something, his scent. Rank.

ANTÔNIO. It must have been the shot.

SARA. No, it was him.

ANTÔNIO. From his clothes?

SARA. No, no, it wasn't his clothes. It was him, himself.

Silence.

ANTÔNIO. Even if someone saw it – no-one did see it – but even if someone did. It was self-defence.

SARA. I know.

Silence.

I was so scared then.

ANTÔNIO. Of him?

She nods.

SARA. I thought I was going to die.

ANTÔNIO. It's over now.

Silence.

There's just one thing that bothers me.

SARA. What?

ANTÔNIO. There could be a bit of trouble to come.

SARA. How come?

ANTÔNIO. Because it was a boy, a child.

SARA. No.

ANTÔNIO. Couldn't there?

SARA. It was self-defence, wasn't it?

ANTÔNIO. Even so.

SARA. No. Nothing's going to happen. Not because it was a child. He was the one who attacked us. We just defended ourselves.

Silence.

That smell – I think it came from his mouth, the mouth of the boy.

Silence.

What time is it?

ANTÔNIO. Almost three. (*Pause.*) Are you sleepy now?

She nods.

Shall we go to bed?

SARA. In a bit.

2.

A long silence.

ANTÔNIO. No-one's trying to intimidate you. We're just talking, that's all, just trying to piece together what it is you might want. To be quite honest with you, we really don't understand what it is you actually saw. None of us knows. We are still very much in the dark about this.

Silence.

Don't you want to say something about . . .

Silence.

What you said on the phone, I – in fact both of us – we were left in a bit of a quandary. I'm not joking.

VÂNIA. I don't even know why I'm here.

SARA. You were the one who sought us out.

VÂNIA *shakes her head.*

Yes, you were, Dona Vânia.

VÂNIA. I didn't go searching for anyone.

SARA. But you called us up on the phone, didn't you? You rang us and told that story of yours. Didn't you?

VÂNIA *nods.*

Well, then.

ANTÔNIO. What is it that you want?

VÂNIA. I – I don't know anything anymore.

ANTÔNIO. But you ought to know.

SARA. It's all right.

Silence.

We only want to help.

ANTÔNIO. Help in whatever way we can. Get this over and
done with. Put a full stop on this story in the easiest way
possible. Finish with this business once and for all.

VÂNIA. Finish?

ANTÔNIO. Yes.

VÂNIA. Finish what exactly? How?

ANTÔNIO. That's what we're all here to find out.

Silence.

VÂNIA. I'm getting out of here.

SARA. Wait, Dona Vânia. Listen to what we have to say –

ANTÔNIO. Leave it. Leave it. It's her right. (*To* VÂNIA.)
If you wish to leave, of course you can go, Dona Vânia,
no-one's going to stop you.

VÂNIA *doesn't move.*

VÂNIA. I don't even know why I came here in the first place.
They told me not to come.

ANTÔNIO. Who?

VÂNIA. Everyone.

ANTÔNIO. Who is it you've been talking to?

VÂNIA. Everyone.

ANTÔNIO. Everyone like who?

VÂNIA. They told me not to come.

ANTÔNIO. But you did.

Silence.

SARA. What is it that you're looking for exactly?

VÂNIA. Nothing. I just wanted to see your faces.

Silence.

SARA. I'll go and get you a glass of water.

VÂNIA. Don't bother yourself on my account.

SARA. I'll get it.

SARA *exits.*

ANTÔNIO (*after a while*). I don't know what you've heard. Maybe someone's told you some kind of lie. But the fact that you're here, in our home, must show you that no-one has anything to hide. The phone call you made left my wife very upset, extremely upset. And me, too. If you want to come and see us, we are here, as you can see. No-one's got anything to hide. All we want is to put paid to this business once and for all. As do you.

There is an uncomfortable silence until SARA *returns at last with the water.*

SARA. There you are.

ANTÔNIO. I was just telling her that you were very upset after the phone call. Isn't that right?

SARA. Yes. Yes, it is.

ANTÔNIO. What you said to us is something very serious.

VÂNIA. Are you now going to say I was lying?

ANTÔNIO. Who was it who told you this story?

VÂNIA. Nobody.

ANTÔNIO. It's going to be very difficult to talk like this.

SARA. We're trying to help, Dona Vânia, really we are.

VÂNIA. You're trying to say I'm lying.

SARA. No, we're not.

VÂNIA. Yes, you are.

Silence.

But it isn't a lie. It's the purest of truths.

SARA. Dona Vânia, all we're trying to say is that you might have got things wrong.

VÂNIA. I know what happened: you killed the boy. Shot him dead, there, by the traffic lights, didn't you? Is that a lie?

Silence.

Is that a lie?

Silence.

ANTÔNIO. If I said it wasn't true, would you believe me?

VÂNIA. No, because I know it is.

ANTÔNIO. And have you got some kind of proof of this?

VÂNIA. Yes, I have.

ANTÔNIO. What?

Silence.

SARA. What, Dona Vânia?

ANTÔNIO. You might have been fooled by someone. Who was it who told you this?

VÂNIA. No-one.

ANTÔNIO. What do you mean, no-one?

VÂNIA. I was there and I saw it for myself.

Silence.

I saw it. No-one told me anything.

ANTÔNIO. And where were you exactly?

VÂNIA. Close by, on the opposite corner.

ANTÔNIO. At that time of night?

VÂNIA *nods.*

And there, from the other corner, you managed to see it was us?

VÂNIA *nods.*

SARA. Dona Vânia –

VÂNIA. I saw it. You know this is no lie. You know. You killed the boy. Shot the boy, killed him.

Silence.

ANTÔNIO. Were you alone?

VÂNIA. There were others with me.

ANTÔNIO. Who?

Silence.

Who, Dona Vânia?

VÂNIA. There were others.

ANTÔNIO. And how did you come to find us?

VÂNIA. I have my ways. And I didn't come here to answer your questions either.

ANTÔNIO. So why did you come here, then?

Silence.

VÂNIA. To see your faces.

ANTÔNIO. Dona Vânia, let's just say for a minute that you were right, that you saw what you saw.

VÂNIA. I did see it.

ANTÔNIO. Fair enough. But understand one thing: you're trying to say that we killed someone.

VÂNIA. I want to go now.

ANTÔNIO. Wait, Dona Vânia, since you're already here, let's talk a bit more. The door is open and you can go at any time you feel like it. But let's talk first. Tell me one thing. You know who we are, but we don't know who you are. Tell me one thing: is the rest of the story all true? Forgive me for asking you this, but we don't know who you are, you see? Is the rest of the story all true?

VÂNIA. What 'rest of story'?

ANTÔNIO. How are we to know if what you said is really true?

VÂNIA. What?

ANTÔNIO. That you're the boy's mother.

VÂNIA. You don't believe me?

SARA. We need to know.

VÂNIA. Do you still remember his name?

SARA. We never knew it.

VÂNIA. It was in the papers.

SARA. Just his initials, not his full name.

VÂNIA. And do you remember them?

ANTÔNIO *nods.*

This is his birth certificate. I've brought it.

ANTÔNIO *examines the document with care.*

And a photo.

SARA *takes a photo and looks at it: she recognises the boy.*

SARA. What's this scar on his face?

VÂNIA. Why do you need to know that?

VÂNIA *takes back the document and photograph.*

Do you believe me now?

Silence.

He was my son.

Silence.

ANTÔNIO. Dona Vânia, please forgive me.

VÂNIA. Forgive you, how? How can someone forgive something like this? I came here to look at your faces. I wanted to see your faces. Don't ask for my forgiveness. Ask God. God is bigger than me.

Silence.

ANTÔNIO. What are you going to do now?

VÂNIA. I don't know. (*Pause.*) Or maybe I do. I'm going to find any justice I can. Yes, I will. Because – Because –

SARA. Have some water.

A long silence. VÂNIA *does not drink.*

VÂNIA. I'm going now.

ANTÔNIO. No, Dona Vânia: stay. You're upset.

VÂNIA. And how would you like me to be?

ANTÔNIO. You're going to go to the police about us, is that it?

Silence.

Dona Vânia, at times like these none of us knows what to say.

Silence.

VÂNIA. I don't think anyone needs to say anything more.

VÂNIA *starts to get ready to leave.*

ANTÔNIO. Dona Vânia.

VÂNIA *stops and turns.*

Sit down, just for one more minute.

VÂNIA. What for?

ANTÔNIO. Please.

VÂNIA *hesitates.*

Please.

VÂNIA *turns and sits down. Silence.*

VÂNIA. Well?

ANTÔNIO. Wait here, I'll be right back.

ANTÔNIO *exits and, while he's away,* SARA *and* VÂNIA *share an uncomfortable silence. Finally,* ANTÔNIO *returns with a pen and a pad.* ANTÔNIO *sits down, opens the pad, thinks for a while and then writes something down. He tears the sheet of paper off the pad and shows it to* VÂNIA.

VÂNIA. What's this supposed to be?

ANTÔNIO. I think you know, don't you?

VÂNIA *shakes her head.*

Yes, you do, Dona Vânia.

Silence.

We will give this amount to you. We will give you this amount and you will forget what happened.

Silence.

It's the only thing we can do, Dona Vânia.

VÂNIA. The boy you killed was my son.

Silence.

ANTÔNIO. It's the only thing we can do for you, Dona Vânia.

VÂNIA. Do you have children?

SARA *shakes her head. Silence.*

ANTÔNIO. It's the only thing we can do. If you go to the police about us, well, you know full well. We'd have to get ourselves a lawyer, we'd have to deal with it.

Silence.

You think you know all about it but you don't. When your son came to the car window, he had a knife.

VÂNIA. No. He didn't have a knife. And the police know this for a fact. There was no knife found on him. There was no knife on him. The police were there and saw for themselves. There was no knife there.

ANTÔNIO. Dona Vânia, what do you have to gain by going to the police about us? You know how things work, don't you? Well, then. Take this money and everyone can rest easy. We feel very bad about what happened, we feel sorry for what happened to your son.

Silence.

VÂNIA. Do you know how old he was? My son – the one you killed.

Silence.

ANTÔNIO. This is what we can give you, Dona Vânia. You can go with me right now to the bank. I'll take this amount of money out and put it in your hand. No-one will mention it again. You don't know me and I don't know you. Our lives go on. What do you say?

Silence.

What do you say?

After a long silence, VÂNIA *nods her head, and there follows another long silence.* ANTÔNIO *checks the time on his watch.*

There's still time to get to the bank. Come with me. We'll settle this right now.

ANTÔNIO *and* VÂNIA *stand up and get ready to leave.*

SARA. Dona Vânia.

VÂNIA *stops at the door and turns back. Silence.*

VÂNIA. What?

SARA. How old was he?

VÂNIA. It was in the papers.

SARA. No, the papers didn't give his age. How old was he, Dona Vânia?

Silence. VÂNIA *does not reply and exits.* ANTÔNIO *leaves with her.*

3.

CÉSAR. I'm sorry about being so late.

ANTÔNIO. It's all right.

CÉSAR. When I set an appointment, I like to keep it. Things like that are very important to me.

ANTÔNIO. Don't worry about it. We understand.

CÉSAR. You spoke to Josias before – someone I know I can trust. He must have explained to you both the way I work – I like to meet a client in their home, see who it is I'm working for, because, as you know, it's getting harder and harder to trust people these days.

ANTÔNIO. Yes, indeed.

CÉSAR (*to* SARA). Don't you agree?

She nods.

But don't worry yourselves that I'm going to start asking you lots of questions. What we're doing here is business, it's work, it's not about idle chit-chat. It's a job of work.

Silence.

Isn't it?

They both nod.

I heard about your story from Josias, and I wanted to find out for myself what was true and what wasn't. I've already started doing things, laying the groundwork, getting it all set up properly. But I need to know what you really want.

ANTÔNIO. You know what all this is about, don't you?

CÉSAR. I've heard the story.

ANTÔNIO. Then you know everything.

CÉSAR. No-one knows *everything*. I know enough, what I need to know, you don't have to worry about giving me any more information. No-one needs to utter a word more about any of this. All I need to know is what you both want from me.

ANTÔNIO. What do you mean?

CÉSAR. You came looking for me, to get something done, I suppose. Now I need to know what that is, from your own mouths, so to speak.

ANTÔNIO. We are like sitting ducks for this woman right now.

CÉSAR. And so?

ANTÔNIO. And so, what we need to know is this: are we in any kind of danger, at risk in any way?

CÉSAR. I got you.

SARA. Can you find out for us?

CÉSAR. This is my job.

ANTÔNIO. Well, that's what we want.

CÉSAR. Just that?

ANTÔNIO. Just that.

CÉSAR. Nothing else?

ANTÔNIO. No.

Silence.

CÉSAR. Fair enough.

ANTÔNIO. When can we expect an answer?

CÉSAR. What about right now?

SARA. Now?

CÉSAR. Yep.

SARA. How come?

CÉSAR. I had an idea what you might want, and as I had some time on my hands and knew you were in a bit of a tight spot, I got down to the job in hand.

SARA. What did you do?

CÉSAR. What I always do. I put myself about a bit, scouted around – same thing I always do.

ANTÔNIO. What did you find out?

CÉSAR. First of all, can you just confirm one thing for me: is this her?

ANTÔNIO *nods.*

I'm showing you this so you don't think I'm some kind of cowboy. This is my job and I take it very seriously indeed.

ANTÔNIO. So what do you think, then?

CÉSAR. I think the danger is only small.

ANTÔNIO. What do you mean 'only small'?

CÉSAR. Very small, then.

ANTÔNIO. And this assumption is based on what exactly?

CÉSAR. On what I've already found out. You're scared she's spent all the money you gave her and she's now going to go running off to the police about the dead boy – her son – isn't that it?

Silence.

Isn't that it? If it's not, just say so.

ANTÔNIO. That's about it, yes.

CÉSAR. Well, then, I went over there and got the gist of this woman, this Vânia person. That's to say, not the woman herself exactly. That's how you do things – the best way is to keep yourself at a bit of a distance.

ANTÔNIO. And what did you find out?

CÉSAR. She's not going to screw you around any more. The boy really was her son, one of those kids who hang out on the streets, just like her in fact. Did she threaten the two of you?

Silence.

But he wasn't her only one. He was the middle child – Ismael.

SARA. Ismael.

CÉSAR. Yeah, the boy. Nice name, don't you think?

Silence.

Anyway, this is how it goes. They've got a house, they're not out on the streets. They're not doing too bad, but they are a bit on the rough side. She's already spent a lot of the money, this Vânia. She did a good job getting that much from you – she'd have taken a lot less, I can tell you, and don't be fooled by any poor-suffering mother act. She'd have run a mile rather than got involved in any kind of legal process. These kind of people have had some experience of being banged up. If you hadn't have given her a centavo, if you'd have got in touch with me sooner, we could have found a way to stamp down on her. It doesn't take much to give these kind of people a fright.

ANTÔNIO. So, then, no-one has anything to worry about.

CÉSAR. The danger is very small. Of course it's there, no-one can be one hundred per cent sure. But this story of the boy, for her, isn't such a big thing. Apart from the ten-year-old she had, there's another one who's twelve, another one who's sixteen who's even worse than the mother if you get my drift, and I think she has a little one and there's another one there who I don't even know if it's really her child or just a friend of the little 'un. But that one was there, too.

Long silence.

ANTÔNIO. Well, I think that's it, then.

CÉSAR. Job done?

ANTÔNIO *nods.*

Happy?

ANTÔNIO *nods.*

Nothing else?

ANTÔNIO. I don't think so.

CÉSAR. Well, I'll be off, then.

ANTÔNIO. Just tell me one thing.

CÉSAR. What?

ANTÔNIO. If anything comes up, can we talk to you again?

CÉSAR. Of course you can.

ANTÔNIO. It's just that it wasn't easy to find you.

CÉSAR. Sometimes it's not so easy, that's true. But that's how the job is. And if I can just say one thing – not that I'm giving you any advice or anything 'cause I ought to know better than that by now, but can I just say one thing. Can I?

ANTÔNIO *nods.*

Look, there are a lot of people out there doing this kind of work, bad people, the kind of people you don't want to get mixed up with. I'm here, in your home, because that's the way I like to work, I need to know who I'm working for, because whatever way you like to look at it, what it all boils down to is I'm in your hands just as you're in mine – trust is what I like to deal in. And I'm saying all this because, believe me, I've seen a lot of stuff go down. I take my work seriously. If I'm not about when you need me, you just have to wait, and when the time comes, give or take a day or so, I'll be there.

Silence.

Even so, it's your life – you have to do what you think is for the best.

ANTÔNIO. No. It's all right. I understand. We can find you again.

SARA. I'm sorry, what was your name again?

Silence.

CÉSAR. You can call me César.

SARA. Mr, er . . . César. Just to get things clear: what is it that could actually still happen?

CÉSAR. It's like I told you before, the danger is minimal. Of course, it's always there. This Vânia could still go crazy and do something, but we can get round it, it's something we can sort out. But if it all blows up during one of those times when I'm away and not contactable, well, there's the problem because these things require a swift solution. You saw how even before we started talking, I was already out there working for you, already doing stuff. Speed is essential.

SARA. And what if it happens?

CÉSAR. Well, there *is* an 'if' there – we just don't know.

Silence.

But I reckon that, as far as your needs are concerned, it's all sorted out.

Silence.

Unless, well, I don't know if this is what you're on about, but I'm only saying it because this is how it is. Unless what you are really telling me, asking me, is if it might be better to do away with this Vânia.

Silence.

In that case, to be honest with you, I'd have to say to you that that would be for the best, but it's your decision, and it's a different job altogether.

Silence.

That I could do.

Long silence.

SARA. I'll leave you two to talk things over, then I'll pop back again.

CÉSAR. I think you should really stay so we just have one conversation. I think your opinion on this matter is very important.

SARA *stays.*

It's your only way of being sure, one hundred per cent. So what do you want?

Silence.

It's not an easy thing to say, eh? Let's do this, I've got a bit of experience of these things: if you want me to sort things out with her, you don't need to say anything because I'll know the answer is yes. Do you want me to put her away?

An extremely long silence.

Fine, then.

He laughs.

Done.

SARA. Why did you laugh just then?

CÉSAR. No reason. Don't worry, you don't need to be afraid of anything any more.

CÉSAR *laughs.*

4.

ANTÔNIO *and* SARA, *cuddled up together, in silence for some time.*

ANTÔNIO. It was much more beautiful than last year, wasn't it? Having the awards there, in the garden, outside. I thought it was beautiful. Everyone in a circle, there in the garden. I thought it was beautiful, a bit different. It was a great idea having it in the garden because it was more peaceful somehow, wasn't it? More open. Better. I loved it. It's the first time they've had it in the garden. The first time. The last time they had it at the entrance to the Great Hall, remember? It was the first time they had it outside. Inside was good, too. They took everything out: those chairs from the entrance, the bureau from reception. They took it all away. The room was left very roomy, very spacious. Very big. But the garden is better, because in the hall, even when it's spacey, it's not the same thing, it's different. Outside it's much – much – much freer, much . . . I loved it. It was beautiful, there in the garden. Everything so well cared for, very beautiful.

Silence.

Did you say something?

She shakes her head.

Silence.

Tired?

She nods.

Me too.

Silence.

My speech, the one I was writing, they talked to me beforehand and asked me not to make it as they wanted the ceremony over with quite quickly, that's why I just said 'thank you very much'.

SARA. Hold me.

He holds her.

They stay like this for a while, holding each other.

What time is it?

ANTÔNIO. Almost three.

SARA. It'll be light soon.

ANTÔNIO. Do you want to go out for breakfast tomorrow, to celebrate the award?

She nods.

SARA. Where?

ANTÔNIO. You choose. It can be my little prize for you.

SARA. So we should go to sleep soon or we'll never wake up early.

ANTÔNIO. Yes.

An extremely long silence.

AT THE TABLE

(*À Mesa*)

Marcos Barbosa

translated into English by Mark O'Thomas

Characters

CASTRO

INÁCIO

BRUNO

THE FATHER

MÁRCIO

LUÍS

Settings: a snack-bar, a dining room, a bar and another snack-bar.

1.

CASTRO *and* INÁCIO, *sat up at the table of a snack-bar.*

CASTRO *has a cup of coffee in front of him and* INÁCIO *is eating, without any discernible pleasure, a piece of cake on a plate.*

CASTRO (*after a pause*). And what about school?

INÁCIO (*almost inaudible*). It's all right.

CASTRO (*not understanding what* INÁCIO *has said*). I didn't get that.

INÁCIO (*a little louder*). It's all right.

CASTRO. Good.

    Silence.

    Getting good marks, getting on well with everyone . . .

    INÁCIO *nods.*

    It's very important, that kind of thing. Studying is just as important as friendships. And what subject do you like the best?

    INÁCIO *thinks for a moment, but in the end shrugs his shoulders.*

    Maths, geography, history . . .

INÁCIO. Maths.

CASTRO. Maths?

    INÁCIO *nods.*

    Me too.

    INÁCIO *stares at* CASTRO *rather incredulously.*

Honestly! Maths and physics. (*After a pause.*) Have you started physics yet?

INÁCIO. No.

CASTRO. Well, I liked both of them. So much so that's how I ended up going into the army – to study engineering. Have a look at this.

He shows INÁCIO *his ring who then looks at it.*

It's from my graduation. Mechanical engineering.

CASTRO *takes the ring off his finger and offers it to* INÁCIO *who looks but does not take it.*

Go on, take it.

INÁCIO *examines the ring.*

Do you want to put it on your finger?

INÁCIO *thinks for a moment and then shakes his head, giving the ring back.*

(*Insisting.*) Go on. Try it on.

INÁCIO *hesitates and then puts the ring on his finger and examines it.*

Let me have a look.

INÁCIO *shows* CASTRO *the ring on his finger.*

Nice. Very nice indeed.

INÁCIO. It's a bit loose.

INÁCIO *takes the ring off and gives it back to* CASTRO.

CASTRO. My father gave it to me.

Silence.

Did you like the cake?

INÁCIO *nods.*

You've hardly eaten a thing.

INÁCIO. I'm not really hungry.

CASTRO. Is that really it – or are you a bit embarrassed?

INÁCIO *smiles with embarrassment.*

You don't need to stand on ceremony for me, you know that, don't you?

INÁCIO *nods.*

Do you or don't you?

INÁCIO *stares at* CASTRO, *puzzled by the repetition of the question.*

(*Insisting.*) Do you or don't you?

INÁCIO. Yes.

CASTRO. Good. Now, then. Let me hear that voice of yours, otherwise I'll end up being the one doing all the talking. It'll be like there's some kind of school lesson going on here.

They both laugh.

You and your brother are really quite alike. Not so much the face. But the way you behave – the way you laugh. He's more talkative of course. You're the quiet one. But that's just how you are, isn't it?

INÁCIO *nods.*

(*Playfully.*) Talk, boy!

INÁCIO. Yes!

CASTRO. That's better!

INÁCIO. I suppose so!

CASTRO. Great!

They both laugh.

They tell me you're a very bright boy, very attentive. Yes, indeed. You're sitting there all quiet, testing me out so I'll end up talking a load of rubbish and at the end of it all you can say 'bye-bye, see you around' and let your brother get on with all the camping stuff.

INÁCIO *laughs.*

Am I right?

INÁCIO. He likes going.

CASTRO. The camping trips?

INÁCIO. Yeah.

CASTRO. Everyone who goes likes it – if they don't mind a bit of rough and tumble. (*After a pause.*) Has he told you what it's like there?

INÁCIO *shrugs his shoulders.*

He must have said something about it.

INÁCIO. He told me to come and talk to you, sir.

CASTRO. To Castro.

INÁCIO *appears not to understand what* CASTRO *is saying.*

To Castro. You don't have to call me 'sir'. (*Playfully.*) We're almost the same age . . .

INÁCIO *laughs.*

(*Still playing.*) What are you laughing at? Isn't it the truth?

They both laugh.

(*After a pause.*) I thought he'd spoken to you, explained what we got up to there, what goes on, what doesn't go on, all that kind of stuff . . .

INÁCIO. No.

CASTRO. But you two are good friends?

INÁCIO *nods.*

He's my helper there. Everyone who goes helps out. One way or another. But as there's a lot of people, I need to have someone who's a bit clever – someone to sort the rabble out, otherwise, if not, well, you know.

Silence.

Your brother is a very helpful lad. A very good lad indeed.
Good as gold. He helps me a lot. That's why I made him a
group leader.

CASTRO *starts to laugh, but then gains control of himself.*

Sorry about that.

INÁCIO. What is it?

CASTRO. Nothing. I just thought of a joke your brother told
me.

Silence.

When your brother told me you wanted to join the group
and go camping with us, I said I wanted to talk to you
beforehand because you can't have just anyone joining up.
It's a beautiful thing we're doing up there, with all the lads,
and I can't and won't have anyone piling in and ruining it.
The door is open but only to those who are good enough.
For those who can really understand our work. Those who
don't like it, leave. Or better still: don't come in the first
place.

Silence.

We talk a lot – me and your brother.

INÁCIO (*after a pause*). Did he say anything about me?

CASTRO *nods.*

What?

CASTRO. That you'd be good for the group, that you're a nice
guy, that you two get on well together . . . Is that true?

INÁCIO *nods.*

Well, we all know how brothers are. There must be fights
now and then, but this is expected, especially at your age.
It's normal.

Silence.

Do you have a girlfriend?

INÁCIO. Me?

CASTRO. Yes, you.

INÁCIO, *a little uncertain, shakes his head.*

Why not?

INÁCIO *shrugs his shoulders.*

There's no girls at camp. We do a lot of hard work – dangerous work. But there are always those girlfriends who want to come along and see what it's all about. You know how girls go on – blaa-dy blaa-dy blaa. There was even one time when it got so bad I had to ban telephone calls. You're at an age for playing around, learning things, having some fun . . . Going out with girls can come later. In the future. Lads these days walk around with their heads turning left, right and centre. That's the crazy kind of world we live in now. (*After a pause.*) Do you want me to order a cup of coffee for you?

INÁCIO. No.

CASTRO. Are you sure?

INÁCIO. I don't like coffee.

CASTRO. No?

INÁCIO *shakes his head.*

They've got soft drinks, too. I didn't offer because I thought it was a bit early for fizzy drinks, but if you'd like . . .

INÁCIO (*after thinking for a moment*). No. Thank you.

CASTRO. Are you sure?

INÁCIO *nods.*

And there's chocolate. Hot chocolate. Everyone says it's very good here. Do you want one?

INÁCIO *shakes his head.*

Nothing?

INÁCIO *shakes his head.*

If you want something, just ask. It's all on the house. You're my guest. I'm going to get another coffee for me anyway as I feel like smoking now. Do you mind if I smoke?

INÁCIO *makes no response.*

(*Checking for the lighter in his pocket before taking it out.*) Don't worry. I'll smoke later.

INÁCIO. No! It doesn't bother me.

CASTRO. Later.

INÁCIO (*insisting*). Honestly. You can smoke.

CASTRO (*putting the lighter away for good*). Even at camp I go out of my way so as not to smoke in front of the lads. So as not to set a bad example. Besides which, you need your breath when you're at camp – there's so much to do, adventures, climbing mountains, fishing, pitching tents, making up campfires . . . Are you prepared for adventure?

INÁCIO *smiles and nods.*

You won't let me down, will you?

Silence.

INÁCIO. Do you have any kids, sir?

CASTRO. 'Sir'?

INÁCIO (*correcting himself*). Do you have any kids?

CASTRO. Three. Two boys and a girl – all grown up now. I'm a granddad now. I've got a little grandson – Guilherme. And another one on the way. But they don't live here. They live far away. You're my sons now – the lads at camp. (*After a pause.*) Why the question?

INÁCIO. Oh, nothing.

CASTRO (*playfully*). I *can* be a bit strict at times, you know? Sorry.

They both laugh.

Well, that won't be a problem with us. Or will it?

INÁCIO. No.

CASTRO. You sure?

INÁCIO *nods.*

Can I trust you?

INÁCIO. Yes.

Silence.

CASTRO. I've had more calls this week from people wanting to join up. A lot of dads come along to enrol their sons. We're getting bigger all the time. This is very good. It's always good to have newcomers. Now, I'm sitting here wondering if it might be a nice idea to have a group of new recruits with you as their leader. (*Seeing* INÁCIO*'s reaction.*) What's wrong? Are you scared?

INÁCIO *shakes his head.*

So, will you do it?

INÁCIO *nods.*

Come on, lad: speak up! Will you do it or not?

INÁCIO. I will.

CASTRO. Louder so I can hear you!

INÁCIO. I will!

CASTRO. That's better! Well done.

INÁCIO (*after a pause*). What does a leader do?

CASTRO. The leader's the one who's in command of a group. He's responsible for checking that everything's all right, if everyone's following the day's orders, and if there's any problem with any of the lads, the leader has a word with me and we – me and you in this case – see what we should or shouldn't do about it, if there needs to be any punishment or whether to let it go . . . Every case is a different case. (*After a pause.*) Have you ever slept in a tent before?

INÁCIO. No.

CASTRO. You'll soon learn. (*After a pause.*) And, to be quite honest, there's no great secret to it. Well, there is one: don't let any rubbish come into the tent. That's all. Things tend to pile up a bit, but apart from that, nothing. The rest is the same as anywhere. Nothing too daunting.

INÁCIO. And what about going to the loo?

CASTRO. What's on your mind?

INÁCIO. How does it work?

CASTRO. There's a proper loo there. And an outhouse with a shower whenever you need it. And there's the river.

Silence.

And what about your mum?

INÁCIO *makes no response.*

Your brother told me. Is she any better?

INÁCIO *nods.*

Your brother had a long chat with me. If you want to talk to me, you needn't keep quiet. You can call on me at camp and we can have a time for us to sit down and chat. Or you can ring me and we can meet up here at the snack-bar or at home – that way I'll be able to introduce you to my wife. You don't need to worry about anything – I know how to keep a secret. All right?

INÁCIO *nods.*

Are you sure you don't want a hot chocolate?

INÁCIO. I think I'll have something fizzy.

CASTRO. What would you like?

INÁCIO. I don't mind.

CASTRO. What would you like?

INÁCIO. What about a Coke?

CASTRO. Of course. (*Getting up after checking the time on his watch.*) You can stay there while I go and get them to bring your drink over. I have to get going now. (*Holding his hand out to* INÁCIO.) Can I count on you being there Friday?

INÁCIO (*shaking* CASTRO's *hand*). Yes.

CASTRO. And do you accept the position as leader of the newcomers?

INÁCIO. I do.

CASTRO. Friday, then.

INÁCIO. Friday.

Just before leaving, CASTRO *stops and goes back to* INÁCIO.

CASTRO. Do you know your way back home on your own?

INÁCIO. Sure.

CASTRO *nods and leaves.* INÁCIO *goes back to the cake.*

2.

INÁCIO, BRUNO *and their* FATHER *at home during dinner.*

FATHER. She's getting better. You're going to have to start helping me out from now on. You don't have to do much. It's just so she doesn't get bothered by anything. If she wants to be on her own, leave her. It does her good. It helps her calm down. Just don't cause her any more worries. (*After a pause, to* INÁCIO.) Did you hear me?

INÁCIO *nods.*

Leave her alone. Her head is already filled with so many things.

BRUNO. Has she decided to start taking the medicine?

FATHER. Yes. She says she's going to.

Silence.

Is it really bad – the soup?

INÁCIO *shakes his head.*

BRUNO. It's good.

FATHER. You've got to eat. If she thinks you don't like it, she'll get upset. She'll get worse. (*After a pause, to* INÁCIO.) Eat your soup.

INÁCIO. I *am* eating it.

FATHER. Is it really bad?

INÁCIO. No.

The three of them go back to their meal.

Silence.

FATHER. When are you going back again?

BRUNO. Going back where?

FATHER. Back to camp.

BRUNO. I think it's the fourteenth. (*To* INÁCIO.) What's the date again?

INÁCIO *makes no response.*

Friday week.

FATHER (*having counted the days*). The fourteenth, then.

BRUNO. Yes.

FATHER. Are you leaving at night?

BRUNO. Late afternoon. About five-ish.

FATHER. And you're back on Sunday?

BRUNO. No, Tuesday.

FATHER. Tuesday?

BRUNO *nods.*

What about school?

BRUNO. We'll be on holiday then.

FATHER. Already?

BRUNO *nods.*

Silence.

INÁCIO. Oh, Dad.

The FATHER *turns to* INÁCIO *but the boy does not say any more.*

FATHER. What's wrong?

INÁCIO. I want to stay behind.

FATHER. Stay behind where?

INÁCIO. At home. I don't want to go to camp.

FATHER. Why not? Weren't you the one walking around saying how good it was?

INÁCIO. I just don't feel like going, that's all.

FATHER. Did something happen?

Silence.

What happened?

BRUNO. Nothing.

The FATHER *continues questioning* INÁCIO *with his gaze.*

INÁCIO. I just don't feel like going any more.

FATHER. And what are you going to do stuck at home?

INÁCIO *does not reply.*

BRUNO. Leave him, dad. He'll change his mind later on.

FATHER. I'm asking you why. If something's happened, I
    need to know about it. I'm the one who sorts out the
    problems here. (*To* INÁCIO.) What happened?

BRUNO. Nothing.

The FATHER *fixes* INÁCIO *with his gaze.*

INÁCIO. Nothing.

BRUNO. See?

FATHER (*to* INÁCIO). If you don't want to go, don't go. Stay.
    I can't force you.

BRUNO. He's going.

INÁCIO. I'm *not* going!

FATHER (*reprimanding him*). Don't shout! Are you mad?

The FATHER's *attention moves to another room: he checks
that all is OK.*

(*To* INÁCIO.) Aren't things bad enough in this house?

Silence.

But just make sure you don't cause any trouble. If you want
to stay home, stay. But on your own. If there's one thing
I won't put up with it's you locking yourself in your room
with your rabble of friends doing God knows what. If you
want to stay home, stay, but you won't bring anyone into
this house.

INÁCIO. Why not?

The FATHER *stares at* INÁCIO.

Dad . . .

FATHER. Are you going to start now?

INÁCIO *does not respond.*

(*To* BRUNO, *after a pause.*) Is there going to be a championship this time?

BRUNO. Yes.

FATHER. What for?

BRUNO. We find out when we get there.

FATHER. But isn't it just the same thing over and over again?

BRUNO. What do you mean?

FATHER. Isn't it your team who always wins?

BRUNO. Last time we lost the fishing contest.

FATHER. Who won that, then?

BRUNO *nods towards* INÁCIO.

Really?

BRUNO. And he's been made leader of his group.

FATHER (*to* INÁCIO, *after a pause*). Is that right, son? Why didn't you tell me?

INÁCIO *makes no response.*

BRUNO. And it was a group of new recruits. Some of them had never even been fishing before.

FATHER (*to* INÁCIO). Congratulations.

INÁCIO *tries to stifle a smile. His* FATHER *ruffles his hair.*

So what's all this about, then?

BRUNO. Leave it, Dad.

FATHER. But he's doing so well . . .

BRUNO. He'll change his mind later on.

FATHER (*leaving the table after some thought*). Wait here.

INÁCIO. Where are you going?

FATHER. I'll be right back.

The FATHER *exits.*

BRUNO (*after a pause*). What's up with you?

INÁCIO. Nothing.

BRUNO. You're not going to start crying again, are you?

INÁCIO. No.

BRUNO. Well, stop it, then. He already thinks something's up.

Some time passes, the FATHER *returns.*

FATHER. What's going on now?

BRUNO. Nothing.

FATHER (*once again, caressing* INÁCIO). What did he do?

INÁCIO (*after some thought*). Nothing.

FATHER (*offering* INÁCIO *something*). Here, it's for you. Look.

INÁCIO *takes an old penknife from his* FATHER.

I've had it since I was a boy but it looks just like new. I had it sharpened a while back.

BRUNO (*trying to get the knife off* INÁCIO). Let me have a look.

INÁCIO *ducks away.*

I only want to see it.

INÁCIO *gives the penknife to his brother who examines it closely.*

It's nice.

INÁCIO. It's mine.

BRUNO. I just said it's nice, that's all.

He gives the penknife back to INÁCIO.

FATHER. It's like new, almost new.

INÁCIO concurs and takes the knife.

Do you like it?

INÁCIO nods.

It's good for fishing, see? To cut the line, for loads of things. It's got a big blade on it. You can use it to clean out fish. And it's got a little saw, did you see that? Ideal for scaling the fish out. Do you like it?

INÁCIO nods.

When you go fishing, at the camp, you can use it.

BRUNO. They'll all be jealous.

FATHER. Tell them it was a present from your dad.

Silence.

(*Again to* INÁCIO.) Do you think there'll be any fishing at the camp this time?

INÁCIO shrugs his shoulders.

BRUNO. Course there will.

FATHER. Really?

BRUNO *nods.*

See? You've already got somewhere you can use it.

They return to their meal.

INÁCIO. Dad . . .

FATHER. What?

INÁCIO does not reply.

What is it, son?

(*To* BRUNO.) What's wrong with him now?

BRUNO. Nothing. Don't you know what he's like?

INÁCIO. Shut up, you!

FATHER (*remonstrating*). Don't shout! (*To* BRUNO.) Did you do something?

BRUNO. Ask him.

FATHER. I'm asking you. Did you or didn't you?

BRUNO. No.

FATHER. Nothing?

BRUNO. Nothing.

The FATHER *fixes* BRUNO *with his gaze.*

(*To* INÁCIO.) Did I do anything?

Silence.

(*To* INÁCIO.) Did I?

INÁCIO *does not respond.*

(*To* FATHER.) See?

FATHER. OK, then. It's over. Done. (*Pushing his plate away.*) That's it now. What's the point in asking you two to help out . . . (*To* INÁCIO.) I think your mum's sleeping in your room. Don't go disturbing her. You can sleep in your brother's room. And you can both do the washing-up. If she wakes up and sees all those dishes, she'll start getting stressed again.

The FATHER *makes to leave but then turns back to talk to* INÁCIO.

And if you don't want the penknife, you can give it back.

He exits.

The two brothers look at each other.

3.

MÁRCIO *and* LUÍS, *in a bar, almost twenty years later.*

MÁRCIO. As soon as I saw you, I recognised you.

LUÍS. Good memory.

MÁRCIO. We used to be friends.

LUÍS. I know. (*After a pause.*) But as years go by, people change. If you hadn't come up to me, I would never have recognised you.

MÁRCIO. You haven't changed much. You used to have long hair. Almost down to your shoulders. Like here. I remember back then I really wanted to grow my hair long but my mother wouldn't let me.

LUÍS. If I see a picture of myself back then, I hardly recognise myself. (*Playfully.*) At least that way I don't have to admit I've got a lot less hair these days.

MÁRCIO. Really?

They both laugh.

Silence.

How long has it been now? Twenty?

LUÍS. No. Less. (*After a quick mental calculation.*) Nearly though.

MÁRCIO. Were you still in contact with him?

LUÍS. No, not at all.

MÁRCIO. Nor me.

LUÍS. You moved away. Whereas we lived in the same area right up until the end. I should never have lost touch with him.

MÁRCIO. True enough.

LUÍS (*after a pause*). You married? Kids?

MÁRCIO. Married, two kids – a boy and a girl.

LUÍS. I've got one.

MÁRCIO. Boy?

LUÍS *nods.*

LUÍS. Yes – Lucas. Three years old.

MÁRCIO. I've got Claudio, four, and Cíntia, seven.

LUÍS. Seven already?

MÁRCIO *nods.*

You married young, then.

MÁRCIO. I didn't have a choice!

They both laugh.

LUÍS *(after a pause)*. How did you hear about the funeral?

MÁRCIO. I got a phone call. A cousin of mine.

LUÍS. I heard by phone as well. Yesterday. Everyone's talking about it.

Silence.

MÁRCIO. So, what's really been going on?

LUÍS. Everyone's got a different theory.

MÁRCIO. When was the last time you two spoke?

LUÍS. A long time ago.

MÁRCIO. When?

LUÍS *(after a pause)*. Back when it was all going on.

MÁRCIO. Never afterwards?

LUÍS *shakes his head.*

Not since we were kids?

LUÍS. No. When it all blew up, a lot of people moved away, his brother disappeared and the shit really hit the fan – they

stoned the snack-bar, my mother made me change schools.
After that, we never really spoke again.

MÁRCIO. After we went to the police?

LUÍS *nods.*

And from then on until now?

LUÍS. Nothing.

Silence.

MÁRCIO. Did you ever report anything?

LUÍS *shakes his head.*

The more that did, the better.

LUÍS. Yes, I'm sure.

MÁRCIO. It ended up being a sort of relief for me. Really,
it was. Even with all the shit that happened. We even had to
move away because of it.

LUÍS. Most people did.

MÁRCIO. We couldn't really stay. They were so ashamed.
My father and my mother. Moving away was for the best.
And what about you?

LUÍS. What?

MÁRCIO. How was it for you – staying on?

LUÍS. We didn't have money to move away. Our whole life
was here. As time went on, things got better.

Silence.

MÁRCIO. You still remember Sílvio?

LUÍS *nods.*

He was our neighbour at the time. We lived in the same
building. On the same floor. One day, his mother came over
crying. It was late at night. I heard the doorbell go and went
to get it. She asked to speak to my mother and then my
mother called my father. She'd found Sílvio was bleeding.
Back then, I didn't even know what the word 'rectum'

meant. But I understood because . . . Because mine had already bled once before. (*After a pause.*) But it wasn't much. I waited a while and then it stopped.

Silence.

LUÍS. She came to our house, too, Sílvio's mother. But I couldn't hear what they were saying. They talked in private. I remember having some sort of conversation with my parents that night, but afterwards, we never really spoke about it again.

MÁRCIO. Sílvio's a pharmaceutical rep now, too. I run into him sometimes.

LUÍS. Oh, really? Do you talk much?

MÁRCIO. About this?

LUÍS *nods.*

(*After a pause.*) No.

Silence.

LUÍS (*checking his watch*). Nine. Ten past nine.

MÁRCIO. It's getting late.

LUÍS. Shall I get the bill?

MÁRCIO. Do you believe this story about suicide?

LUÍS. Everyone says something different.

MÁRCIO. But what do you make of it?

LUÍS. I think it was an accident. His father had no reason to lie.

Silence.

MÁRCIO. But do you think there could be more to it than that?

LUÍS. Like what?

MÁRCIO *does not reply.*

After all these years?

MÁRCIO *shrugs his shoulders.*

No. You're still here. And me. And Sílvio. And all the others. We all grew up and we're living our lives now. We're getting on with it. What's passed is passed.

Silence.

Why the question?

MÁRCIO. No reason.

LUÍS. Did you ever – Did you think about it? Killing yourself?

MÁRCIO. There was a time, back then, when I found my mother at home, hidden away, crying. And I knew it was because of all this. And there was another time, after I'd moved schools, some kid made a joke. I remember at that time I really wanted to die.

LUÍS. That's something else.

MÁRCIO. I know.

LUÍS. You were just a kid.

MÁRCIO. I know.

Silence.

LUÍS. There are times when we all think about dying.

MÁRCIO. Of course there are.

LUÍS. It's just, the way you say it . . .

MÁRCIO (*cutting in*). It's just a manner of speaking.

Silence.

Bruno, his brother, the one who disappeared, he raped me too, you know. More than once. (*After a pause.*) Did he get you, too?

LUÍS *nods.*

Silence.

LUÍS. Did you see his father there at the cemetery? They said he was ill but I didn't realise just how bad he was. And his

wife passed away a little while ago. Just a while ago. Last
year. Sad, isn't it? Now he's got no-one. His wife dies and
then his son soon afterwards…

MÁRCIO. That other son of a bitch is still out there though.

LUÍS. No-one ever heard any more about Bruno as far as
I know.

MÁRCIO. But the father must know something.

LUÍS. He might do.

MÁRCIO. He knows. Of course he knows.

LUÍS. I can only imagine what must be going through his head
right now. Now that I'm a father, I ask myself what it must
be like to lose a son.

MÁRCIO. I think I'd be very angry.

LUÍS. Who with?

MÁRCIO. I don't know… But don't you know what I mean?

LUÍS *nods without much conviction.*

LUÍS. I think I'd be very tired, exhausted, with no strength. If
you ask me: tired of what? I really don't know either.

MÁRCIO. It's tough.

LUÍS. Do you have something against the father?

MÁRCIO. Why?

LUÍS. No reason. Just the way you're talking about him, about
Bruno…

MÁRCIO. No. Not really.

LUÍS. The father had a son in exactly the same situation as us.

MÁRCIO. And he was our friend.

LUÍS. And he was our friend.

MÁRCIO. I have no feelings of anger against his father at all.
Honestly. I'm a father too, I know what it's like.

LUÍS. And, what's done is done: it's over now. No-one talks about it any more or has any reason to.

MÁRCIO. True enough.

Silence.

Back then, I was ashamed. Afterwards, I started to feel angry, but now… I don't know. When my cousin told me Inácio had died, that maybe he'd killed himself, I jumped in my car and drove here straight away. We hadn't seen each other for years, since it all happened or just afterwards, but he used to be my friend. Just as you are my friend. And even with all the shit that happened, one way or another, even after all this time, I can see that we were all together, all of us. And still are. (*After a pause.*) I wish they'd left the coffin open so I could have seen his face. I liked him.

Silence.

LUÍS *checks his watch.*

Sometimes I stop and think. There are some things you just can't explain. His brother's the one who should be in a coffin. At least the old queer was put away. Bruno didn't even get that.

LUÍS. He wasn't even seventeen at the time.

MÁRCIO. So fucking what?

Silence.

LUÍS. I'd better get going.

MÁRCIO. Did you know the old queer was released?

LUÍS *nods.*

I only heard about it just over a month ago.

LUÍS. He's been out for years.

MÁRCIO. Years?

LUÍS *nods.*

When?

LUÍS *shrugs his shoulders.*

Silence.

LUÍS. He changed his name.

MÁRCIO. How did you hear that?

LUÍS. I just heard.

MÁRCIO. So what's his name now, then?

LUÍS (*after a pause*). That I don't know.

Silence.

MÁRCIO. If none of us had gone ahead and reported what was going on, he'd still be there now.

LUÍS *goes to say something but* MÁRCIO *interrupts him.*

I'm not angry with you, or feel any spite or anything. Some of us reported it, some of us didn't. That's how it was. Only you can say where the shoe squeezes your foot. I'm not saying anything.

LUÍS. And all I'm saying is that, for me, this whole thing is over. (*Looking at his watch.*) I really should be making a move. I'll get the bill . . .

MÁRCIO (*cutting in*). Did you ever... There at the camp, did you – Did you, with another boy, the way that they said?

LUÍS *does not reply.*

Did you?

LUÍS *nods.*

With me?

A long silence.

LUÍS. I'm sorry.

MÁRCIO. When I saw your face, I – It all came flooding back to me.

LUÍS. Back then –

LUÍS *does not finish his sentence.*

MÁRCIO. It's all right. I mean it. It's all right.

LUÍS. We were just kids.

MÁRCIO. I know. All right.

Silence.

LUÍS. We were friends.

MÁRCIO. We *are* friends.

LUÍS. We are friends.

MÁRCIO. We are.

Silence.

LUÍS. Sorry.

MÁRCIO. Leave it.

Silence.

I did it, too.

Silence.

Why didn't we stop them before, eh? What the hell were we so afraid of?

LUÍS. I think we were never really afraid.

MÁRCIO. What do you mean?

Silence.

LUÍS *checks his watch.*

Shall we go?

LUÍS. Yes. Let's go.

MÁRCIO. I'll get the bill.

LUÍS. No. You're the out-of-town visitor. I'll get it.

MÁRCIO. No, I invited you.

LUÍS. I insist.

MÁRCIO. Are you sure?

LUÍS. Absolutely.

    LUÍS *signals to the waiter for the bill.*

MÁRCIO. You've got my card, I've got yours. We'll stay in contact with each other.

LUÍS. Sure.

MÁRCIO. And, please, let's not lose touch.

LUÍS. No. Whatever happens. One day, we'll arrange to meet up somewhere. You can come over to my place or me yours.

MÁRCIO. Yes. One day.

    Silence.

LUÍS. So how's life for a pharmaceutical rep these days?

MÁRCIO. It's shit.

    They both laugh.

LUÍS. Let your hair grow. Maybe it'll suit you better.

MÁRCIO. There was a time I did. But that was shit too!

    Again, they laugh.

    LUÍS *checks to see if the waiter is on his way with the bill: Not yet.*

    If you ever bumped into him, what would you do?

LUÍS. What do you want me to say?

MÁRCIO. Just be honest.

    LUÍS *does not reply. He then laughs quite suddenly.*

    What's so funny?

LUÍS. Nothing.

MÁRCIO. You wouldn't do anything, would you?

LUÍS. What do you care?

MÁRCIO. I don't.

LUÍS. So why ask, then?

MÁRCIO. You say it's all over. Over.

LUÍS. It is.

MÁRCIO. Right. (*After a pause.*) Let's just hope some AIDS-case raped him. That they fucked him hard with a broomstick and all that other stuff that goes on in prisons. (*After a pause.*) If I ever run into that scum, I – I don't know.

LUÍS. You've got your own life to take care of. You've got your family.

MÁRCIO. That's right.

Silence.

And besides I've already done my bit.

4.

LUÍS *and* CASTRO *in a snack-bar which is reminiscent of the one in the first scene, some weeks later.*

CASTRO. You can imagine what it must have been like for my family at the time. My kids – even though they live far away – suffered a lot. All of them. Without exception. The eldest was pregnant back then and she nearly lost the baby. It was touch and go for a while. My wife, who still needs medical assistance even today, is undergoing very serious treatment and doesn't need any more stress. On the contrary, in fact. And I've done all I can to keep her going. What I'm able to do and what I'm not able to do. And if needs be, I'll do more. I'd do even more because a marriage like ours is something quite rare. Very rare. These days everything gets thrown away. Everything is thrown out. But us, my wife and I, we've been together for so long, a very long time. And it's about love at the end of the day, which is something quite rare these days. And every day of my life, every day that I live, I take on my responsibility to look after her, take care of her, as she takes care of me. (*After a pause.*) We've already found ourselves a lawyer and he's told us that if we want to, we can take some legal action for the losses I incurred and damages, or whatever it's called, one way or another that's what we could do, but she doesn't want it because she doesn't want to upset anyone. Nor do I. That's why we let things lie. That's why we left all that we had and came here, to live in peace. We knew how to forgive. But it's good that everyone knows that I've still got the right to sue anyone who threatens me, from back then, who insults me – me or my family. It's my right. Our right. And at the same time as it's in our hearts not to go and complicate anyone's life, we want to live in peace. That's all we want: to live in peace. Me, my wife, my family.

Silence.

How did you find me?

LUÍS *does not answer.*

This snack-bar isn't held in my name, I'm not in the phone book, nothing like that . . . And apart from that you came all the way from another state. How did you find me?

LUÍS *does not answer.*

Now and then, one of you shows up. If they come and find me, they do so illegally. Spying on someone is illegal, I don't know if you're aware of that. Using a private detective or the services of some bent police officer are all crimes, you know. It's not that I'm threatening anyone. It's not that at all. Besides, as you've seen: you arrived and I opened both the door of my house and my workplace to you. You are very welcome. I always wished you all well, those from the camp, and still do. You can be quite sure of that.

Silence.

Do you know how most of them come here? (*After a pause.*) With hate in their hearts. So, now tell me: why is that?

LUÍS *does not answer.*

Why?

LUÍS *does not answer.*

I helped you all, as much as I could, back then. Each and every one of you. I looked after you like you were my own. The boy that died – what was his name? – (*Remembers.*) Inácio. He was one of the ones who needed me. Me and my wife. To give him a father's touch, a mother's touch. We did all that for him.

Silence.

Everything that happened . . . Happened. But what nobody is saying is the truth – is that at no time did I ever wish any harm to come to anyone. You know what I mean. I never did anything to hurt any of you. Never. You know that. I treated you all with love. Love is a rare thing these days. I never taught you to be disloyal to each other. Never. I always taught you to respect your elders, to love your

parents, your brothers and sisters. Always. You were there.
You went through the whole thing. You saw it for yourself.

Silence.

The way they talked about me afterwards . . . But my
conscience is clear. I am not someone of bad character,
never have been. Even today – do you see this place? I've
got my business, I pay my taxes, I help people out around
here, I'm a good neighbour . . . You can ask around when
you leave. They're building a playing field just around the
back for the local kids to play – and who's funding the
construction? Me. I run football championships for the lads,
I help out in so many ways. Everyone's very grateful to me
around here. You ask anyone. Seeing the kids grow up,
making something of themselves, gives me a lot of pleasure.
I go out there, on the veranda, and look at them. My heart
full of joy, it's really amazing. Are you a father yet?

LUÍS *nods.*

Have you got a son?

LUÍS *nods.*

How old is he?

LUÍS (*after a pause*). Three.

CASTRO. So, you can understand what I'm saying. You're
    intelligent, sensitive. Always were. You must be able to
    understand the joy of seeing a young boy grow up, coming
    into bloom, changing from a baby to a boy, from a boy to a
    young lad, from a lad to an adult . . . It's one of God's
    miracles.

Silence.

I'm sorry for talking like that. It's just I can see in your face
that you're a man with a good heart. You're someone I can
talk to. You understand. (*After a pause.*) Would you like
another coffee?

LUÍS *shakes his head.*

There's soft drinks, water . . . Would you like something?

LUÍS *shakes his head.*

The hot chocolate here's very good, too. Everyone says so. Would you like one?

LUÍS *does not reply. He lights a cigarette.*

I'm going to make an exception in your case because it's empty now, but I don't as a rule like people smoking in here. It sets a bad example to the young people. It'll start to fill up soon. There's a school nearby and the lads come in to play on the pinball machine after their classes, have a drink, play . . .

LUÍS *continues smoking his cigarette.* CASTRO *looks back at him.*

I might as well make the most of the place being empty and keep you company. Can I borrow your lighter?

LUÍS *gives the lighter up to* CASTRO *who takes a cigar out of his pocket, lights it and starts smoking.*

You don't mind, do you?

LUÍS *does not answer.*

You weren't one of those who reported me, were you?

LUÍS *does not answer.*

Were you?

They remain like that, for a while, smoking until suddenly LUÍS *puts his cigarette out and gets up.*

You off already?

5.

Following on from Scene 2.

BRUNO. Did you have to?

INÁCIO *does not reply.*

Haven't I told you how it is? Didn't I say there was no problem about it?

INÁCIO *does not reply.*

This is stupid… (*After a pause.*) Are you angry?

INÁCIO *does not reply.*

It was only that once. You're a leader now. It's over and done with. It didn't even hurt or anything.

Silence.

If you don't want to again, fine. No problem. Now you're a leader. If you don't want to, you don't have to. (*After a pause.*) It was worse for me – I had to stand everyone taking the piss out of me because you beat me in the fishing contest.

INÁCIO *laughs.*

Come on, finish your soup so we can put the table away. It's disgusting, this soup.

INÁCIO *does not have any more soup, he just stares at his brother.*

Dad's all wound up right now. If you don't want the soup, don't have it. Throw it away, while he's not looking. But don't piss him off. If he loses his temper, he'll end up taking us both out of the camp. Do you really want to leave?

INÁCIO *does not reply.*

Well, then… You've got to stop all this nonsense. You are a man, aren't you?

INÁCIO *does not reply.*

(*Under his breath.*) You're like a little girl…

INÁCIO *suddenly flings the penknife at* BRUNO *who deflects it.*

(*Getting up to retaliate.*) Are you mad?

INÁCIO (*calling out*). Dad!

BRUNO *stops immediately.*

Dad!

The FATHER *enters.*

FATHER. What's going on now?

INÁCIO *does not respond.*

What's going on now?

INÁCIO. Something did happen at the camp.

Silence.

A Nick Hern Book

Almost Nothing / At the Table first published in Great Britain
as a paperback original in 2004 by Nick Hern Books Limited,
14 Larden Road, London W3 7ST in association with
the Royal Court Theatre, London

Cover Image: Matthew Mawson

Typeset by Country Setting, Kingsdown, Kent, CT14 8ES
Printed and bound in Great Britain by Bookmarque, Croydon, Surrey

A CIP catalogue record for this book is available from
the British Library

ISBN 1 85459 790 6